# To the Bird Lover

An old story relates that Columbus discovered the New World thanks to parrots. Just as he was about to give up the search, he took the advice of his captain to follow the colored birds that were flying in the sky. These were not seabirds but birds of the forest that were flying toward land. And so, on October 12, 1492, Columbus landed on an uninhabited island in Central America that contained sycamore trees alive with flocks of screaming parrots.

Parrots have lived in human captivity for more than 2000 years. They have been kept because of their communicative nature, beautiful plumage, interesting behavior, and unusual ability to imitate. Also, they often develop a great attachment to human beings. Anyone who befriends a parrot gains a friend for life. Although parrots are very popular, people often know too little about them to care for them properly.

This little book on parrots and parakeets provides you with a very helpful introduction. With fascinating color photographs it introduces 58 species that are offered by dealers or can be encountered in a zoo. A short, descriptive text tells about their native habitat, appearance, living conditions in the wild and in captivity, and indicates which species are endangered. This information is rounded out by the chapter ''General Information about Parrots'' (pp. 61–62). This handy pocket guide is the ideal companion for shopping in a pet store, a walk through the zoo, or a visit to a bird sanctuary.

The author and the editors of *Barron's Mini Fact Finders* wish you much pleasure in becoming acquainted with parrots and parakeets and learning to identify them.

## Important Note

People who suffer from an allergy to feathers or feather dust should not keep parrots. If there is any doubt, check with your doctor before you get one. In dealing with parrots, you can be bitten or scratched. Have such injuries attended by a doctor immediately. Psittacosis (parrot fever) is not a common ailment of parrots, but it can occasionally produce life-threatening symptoms in people and parrots. Therefore, go to the doctor without fail if you have symptoms of cold or flu.

Photograph on front cover: green-winged macaw; back cover: budgerigars (parakeets).

# How to Use this Book

This *Barron's Mini Fact Finder* presents the most common and most popular members of the parrot family. Colored photographs show the features most important for identification. A brief descriptive text tells about the parrots' appearance, native habitat, living conditions in the wild, and care in captivity. It makes identification easy even for the beginner.

## Explanation of the Color Code
You can tell at a glance whether the species being described is suited for indoor cage living or only for an outdoor aviary by looking at the colored bar on the upper side of the photograph.

▬▬▬  Easy to keep and breed in a room cage

▬▬▬  Outdoor aviary recommended; if kept indoors, roomy cage and supervised free flight

▬▬▬  Suited only for keeping in outdoor aviary

## Explanation of Abbreviations
*L*, length; *M*, male; *F*, female; *SS*, subspecies; *B*, length of brooding period; *N*, length of nesting period; *I-XII*, the months in which brooding occurs in the native habitat.

## Explanation of Descriptive Text
The common English name is given above the picture. Sometimes a second name that is used just as widely is given.
The **Scientific Name** is listed below the picture. Distribution and habitat are listed under the heading **Habitat.** Size and characteristic features are described under the heading **Characteristics.** The heading **Life in the Wild** gives information about brooding, raising the young, and social behavior in the natural environment. The requirements for a proper life in captivity are explained under the headings **Care** and **Feeding.** Behavior patterns in captivity are indicated under the heading **Behavior.** The **Remarks** note endangered species, likelihood of breeding, and other pertinent information.

## The author
Dr. Kurt Kolar, zoologist, behavior researcher, and breeder of small parrots, is the author of many successful parrot books.

# Moluccan Cockatoo

**Scientific Name:** *Cacatua moluccensis*
**Habitat:** Forested regions. Southern Moluccas.
**Characteristics:** L 20½ in (52 cm). M and F white, salmon-pink tinge. Iris in M black, in F dark brown.
**Life in the Wild:** Nests in high tree hollows; 2 eggs, B 30 days, N 90 days, III/IV. Searches for food in coconut plantations and grain fields.
**Care:** Aviary cage of strong wire mesh with a heatable sheltered area. For tame animals cage of about 1 cu yd (1 m³)
in size. Allow to be free on a stand under supervision. Branches and roots for gnawing. Regular spraying with lukewarm water hinders development of too much feather dust. Will destroy most cages.
**Feeding:** Sunflower seeds, wheat, corn, oats, peanuts, pine nuts, fruit.
**Behavior:** Close pair bonding. Tame single birds choose a special person to relate to. Loud voice (contact calls).
**Remarks:** Endangered by persecution and capture. To date only rarely bred.

**Scientific Name:** *Cacatua sulphurea*

**Habitat:** Open rain forests below 1640 ft (500 m). Celebes and Buton (Indonesia).

**Characteristics:** L 13 in (33 cm). White. Yellow ear spot; crest feathers yellow, orange in one SS. Undersides of wings yellowish. Iris in M dark brown, in F reddish brown. 6 SS.

**Life in the Wild:** Brooding period dependent on rainy season. Nests in tree hollows; 2–4 eggs, B 28 days, N 65 days, IX–XI. Follow civilization.

**Care:** Metal aviary with frost-free sheltered area. Only tame birds are suitable for keeping indoors (large cage, supervised freedom on a stand). Bathe in the rain or under a shower.

**Feeding:** Sunflower seeds, corn, wheat, millet, pine nuts, berries, fruit, green food.

**Behavior:** Enjoy contact with one another, very aggressive toward other birds.

**Remarks:** Abundant species. Breeding usually successful. Mount nest boxes in dark cage or aviary corners.

# Galah or Roseate Cockatoo

**Scientific Name:** *Eolophus roseicapillus*

**Habitat:** Open country. Interior of Australia.

**Characteristics:** L 13½ in (35 cm). Forehead and crest white; bridle, cheeks, and underside of body rose red; upper side gray. Iris in M dark brown, in F reddish. 2 SS.

**Life in the Wild:** Nests in tree hollows; 3–5 eggs, B 25 days, N 50 days; II–V (north), VII–I (south). Follows civilization.

**Care:** Metal cage with un-heated sheltered area. Tame animals also in large parrot cages with supervised freedom. Food is taken from the ground.

**Feeding:** Sunflower seeds, oats, wheat, millet, fruit, green food.

**Behavior:** Loud voices, as in many other parrots that live in flocks. Compatible with other large species in aviaries. Leaves and twigs are carried into the brooding box.

**Remarks:** Treated as pests in Australia. In recent times breeding has met with regular success.

# Goffin's Cockatoo

**Scientific Name:** *Cacatua goffini*

**Habitat:** Forests. Tanimbar island (Indonesia).

**Characteristics:** L 12½ in (32 cm). White. Bridle and base of head and crest feathers salmon-pink. Iris in M dark brown, in F reddish.

**Life in the Wild:** Broods in tree hollows; 2–3 eggs, B 28 days, N 90 days, I–XII. Disappearing locally because of deforestation.

**Care:** Metal aviary at least 13 feet (4 m) long with temperate sheltered area. Provide warmth, high humidity, partial shade, and materials for gnawing.

**Feeding:** Sunflower seeds, canary grass seed, wheat, oats, corn, carrots, apples, green food. Especially likes corncobs and millet spray.

**Behavior:** Loud cries. In courtship M throws himself forward, bows deeply before F, and struts about, crying at the top of his voice.

**Remarks:** Endangered species. Imported in larger numbers since 1972. Breeding in captivity desperately needed.

# Violet-necked Lory

**Scientific Name:**
*Eos squamata squamata*
**Habitat:** Rain forests. Schildpad island; western Papuan islands.
**Characteristics:** L 10 in (25 cm). M and F red. Broad band on throat and nape; greater wing coverts and primaries blackish. 7 SS.
**Life in the Wild:** Broods in tree hollows; 2 eggs, B 26 days, N 70 days. Feeds on nectar, pollen, insects, and fruit.
**Care:** Aviary at least 6½ ft (2 m) long with frost-free sheltered area. Facilities for bathing. All lories spray their droppings; therefore, set up the interior enclosure with walls that can be washed easily. Maintaining a cage indoors is not possible.
**Feeding:** Baby food gruel, honey, flower pollen, multivitamin preparations, commercially prepared lory food, fruit, some sunflower seed kernels (sprouted if possible).
**Behavior:** Very loud cries for contact between mates.
**Remarks:** Abundant species. Breeding possible. Spread nest boxes with wood shavings.

**Scientific Name:** *Trichoglossus haematodus moluccanus*

**Habitat:** Forested regions. Eastern Australia, Tasmania, Torres Strait islands.

**Characteristics:** L 11½ in (29 cm). M and F head and belly violet-blue. Greenish yellow band on nape, otherwise upper side green. Breast yellow to orange-red. One of 24 SS of many-colored lories.

**Life in the Wild:** Broods in tree hollows; 2 eggs, B 25 days, N 56 days. Sedentary birds in rain forests, otherwise nomadic. Searches for food (flowers, seeds, fruit, ripened grain) in company with other lories.

**Care:** Aviary with frost-free sheltered area. Facilities for bathing and perching. Does not get along with other species.

**Feeding:** Like violet-necked lory; also soft food, mealworms.

**Behavior:** After brooding period lives in large flocks; common roosting trees. Avoids ground; prefers to bathe in damp foliage or in rain.

**Remarks:** Abundant species. May be bred without difficulties for generations.

**Scientific Name:** *Lorius garrulus garrulus*
**Habitat:** Forested regions. Halmahera and Weda (Indonesia).
**Characteristics:** L 12 in (30 cm). M and F glowing red. Front edge of wing and spot between wing and neck yellow. Wings and thigh green. Primary feathers gray underneath with reddish band, otherwise undersides of wings yellow. 3 SS.
**Life in the Wild:** Broods in tree hollows; 2 eggs, B 26–28 days, N 75 days, VI–IX. Pairs live in their own territories.

**Care:** If possible keep in pairs; temperature not below 50° F (10° C). Becomes very tame; great talent for imitation; therefore, keeping of a single bird is wrong for this species. Provide facilities for bathing.
**Feeding:** Like the violet-necked Lory; also fruit, white sunflower seed kernels.
**Behavior:** Aggressive toward other pairs of the same species and (tame birds) toward the caretaker. Loud voices.
**Remarks:** Abundant species. Breeding necessary for preservation of the stock.

**Scientific Name:**
*Trichoglossus goldiei*
**Habitat:** Mountain forests. New Guinea.
**Characteristics:** L 7½ in (19 cm). M and F green; yellowish green striped undersides. Forehead and crown red; bridle and cheek region violet-pink; light ring around eyes.
**Life in the Wild:** Broods in tree hollows; 2 eggs, B 23–25 days, N 65 days. Gathers in small groups in crowns of trees, where nectar, pollen, insects, and fruit are consumed.
**Care:** Aviary with heatable sheltered area. Do not allow temperature to fall below 50° F (10° C). With appropriate precautions against the considerable fouling, keeping in a cage is also possible.
**Feeding:** Puree; nectar for hummingbirds; soft, sweet fruit (see also violet-necked lory).
**Behavior:** Constant mood calls between mates. Less "playful" than other lories. Less loud.
**Remarks:** Not endangered but a somewhat rare species. Breeding is ordinarily successful. Clean nest boxes frequently.

**Scientific Name:** *Lathamus discolor*

**Habitat:** Wooded savannas, gardens, parks. Tasmania.

**Characteristics:** L 9½ in (24 cm). Green. Forehead, throat, lower wing coverts red; bridle yellow; crown blue. F duller.

**Life in the Wild:** Often broods in communities in eucalyptus trees; 2–5 eggs, B 20 days, N 35 days, IX–XII. Searches for food (nectar, fruit, seeds, insects) in flocks.

**Care:** Aviary with flight length of 13 ft (4 m). Sensitive to frost. Offer feed on a high table.

**Feeding:** Fruit; soft feed; puree (baby food, honey); half-ripe, soaked, or sprouted seeds.

**Behavior:** Lively and sociable. Several pairs will tolerate each other. Gets acclimated quickly.

**Remarks:** Abundant species. Sometimes also called swift lory but is not related to lories. Can be bred. Overwinters in southeastern Australia. Apparently moves at night. (Picture shows immature bird.)

# Red-fronted Kakariki

**Scientific Name:**
*Cyanoramphus novaezelandiae*
**Habitat:** Forests. New Zealand and adjacent islands.
**Characteristics:** L 11½ in (29 cm). Green. Front of head and spot behind the eye red. F with smaller head and red spot. 9 SS, of which 2 are extinct.
**Life in the Wild:** Nests in tree hollows; also makes island-shaped nests in rock crevices and in the earth; 5–10 eggs, B 20 days, N 30 days, X–XII. The SS in the Antipodes islands live among penguins.
**Care:** Keep in pairs or in fami-

ly groups. Likes to scratch on the ground, hence in danger of worm infestations. Likes to bathe. Using tiles with grass between them on the enclosure floor gives the animals something to do.
**Feeding:** Grain mixtures for large parrots, sprouted and soaked seeds, soft food (bread with milk), green food, apples, carrots.
**Behavior:** Climbs on cage without using beak. Does not gnaw wood. Voice tolerable.
**Remarks:** Endangered species. Easy to breed.

**Scientific Name:**
*Melopsittacus undulatus*
**Habitat:** Open grassland with few trees. Australia.
**Characteristics:** L 7 in (18 cm). Green. Forehead and cheeks yellow. Back horizontally banded with black and yellow. Cere in M blue, in F brown. Many mutations. Most common Australian species.
**Life in the Wild:** Nests in tree hollows. Brooding period dependent on food supply (rainy season); 4–8 eggs, B 18 days, N 30 days; VII–I (south), VI–IX (north). In dry spells millions of budgerigars congregate in watery areas.
**Care:** If possible keep in pairs; species is not suited for single living. Large cage with appropriate mesh gauge. Daily free flight in the room.
**Feeding:** Millet, canary grass seed, oats; iodine for indoor birds.
**Behavior:** Sociable. Young birds quickly become tame. Dolls and other toys serve as substitute partners.
**Remarks:** First imported in 1840. Today the most common bird species in human captivity.

**Scientific Name:** *Neophema pulchella*

**Habitat:** Open forested regions. Southeastern Australia.

**Characteristics:** L 8 in (20 cm). M face and wing coverts turquoise. Underside yellow. Brown-red shoulder spot. F paler, less blue on face.

**Life in the Wild:** Nests in holes in trees; 4–7 eggs, B 19 days, N 28 days, VIII–XII. Finds food on the ground.

**Care:** Keep in pairs. Gets along well with grass finches (zebra finches, Gouldian finches, etc.). Aviary 6½ to 10 ft (2–3 m) long. Protection from cold and dampness necessary.

**Feeding:** Millet, canary grass seed, some hemp and niger seed, sunflower seed kernels; fruit, carrots, green food.

**Behavior:** Likes to be on the ground; good flier. Does not gnaw. Melodious voice. Because of aggressivness of M, pairing is sometimes difficult.

**Remarks:** Not endangered but rather rare. Easy to breed; young very wild after leaving the nest. Equip aviary fencing with camouflage (branches, etc.).

# Splendid Grass Parakeet

**Scientific Name:** *Neophema splendida*

**Habitat:** Arid bush country. Interior southern Australia.

**Characteristics:** L 8 in (20 cm). M green back, yellow belly, red throat and upper breast, blue face. F with green breast, pale blue head. Several mutations.

**Life in the Wild:** Nests in acacias hollows; 3–5 eggs, B 19 days, N 28 days, VIII–XII. Little need for water. Quiet birds; like to conceal themselves in underbrush.

**Care:** Aviary 6½ to 10 ft (2–3 m) long. Needs room to fly, otherwise becomes fat. Sensitive to cold and dampness. Enclosure can be planted. Likes to bathe in sand.

**Feeding:** Millet, canary grass seed, hemp, niger seed, sunflower seed kernels, weed seeds, nuts, vegetables, and fruit.

**Behavior:** Gets along with other bird species. F transports leaves in rear feathers. Sunbathes with wings extended.

**Remarks:** Susceptible to worm infestations. Was considered extinct for 90 years.

**Scientific Name:**
*Neophema bourkii*
**Habitat:** Sandy prairies with acacia bushes. Central Australia.
**Characteristics:** L 8 in (20 cm). M olive brown on upper side. Bright blue forehead, stripe over the eyes, upper and undertail coverts, rump. Throat and breast feathers brownish with pink edge. Belly bright pink. F without blue forehead stripe.
**Life in the Wild:** Nests in tree hollows; 4–5 eggs, B 18 days, N 28 days, VIII–XII. Will also come into gardens.

**Care:** Aviary 6½ to 10 feet (2–3 m) long. Warmth and dryness required. Bathes in rain or under a spray.
**Feeding:** Millet, canary grass seed, some niger and hemp, sunflower seed kernels, fruit, green food, yeast, boiled rice.
**Behavior:** Gets along with small birds. No social grooming. Soft voice. Doesn't gnaw. Active in the evenings.
**Remarks:** Long thought to be extinct. Very abundant today. Especially recommended for beginners. Easy to breed.

**Scientific Name:** *Psephotus haematonotus*
**Habitat:** Grasslands with some trees; water in the vicinity. Southeastern Australia.
**Characteristics:** L 11 in (28 cm). M bluish green. Nape and breast bright green. Red rump. Primaries and edge of wing blue. Black beak. F plumage gray-olive-green; gray beak. 2 SS. Blue and yellow mutations.
**Life in the Wild:** Nests in tree hollows; 4–7 eggs, B 19–20 days, N 30 days, VIII –XII. Often in the company of rosella parakeets and galahs in farmlands. Follows civilization. Moves in flocks after the brooding period.
**Care:** Aviary at least 6½ ft (2 m) with dry sheltered area. Facilities for bathing.
**Feeding:** Mixed seeds, sunflower seeds, green food, corncobs, apples, carrots.
**Behavior:** Pairs stay together all year long. Tolerable voice. Does not gnaw.
**Remarks:** Abundant species. Easy to keep and to breed.

**Scientific Name:** *Psephotus varius*

**Habitat:** Dry grassland and bush country. Central and southern Australia.

**Characteristics:** L 10½ in (27 cm). M bluish green. Yellow forehead, red crown. Yellow and orange belly. Median wing coverts yellow. Primaries, secondaries, and edge of wing blue. Dark gray beak. F olive green. Median wing covert red (different from F red-rumped parakeet). Beak brownish gray. Coloration of M varies.

**Life in the Wild:** Nests in tree hollows; 3–6 eggs, B 20 days, N 35 days, VII–XII. Brooding F will allow herself to be touched. Mostly finds food on the ground.

**Care:** Cage at least 6½ ft (2 m) long. Provide space protected against cold and dampness.

**Feeding:** Mixed grains for large parrots, sprouted and half-ripe seeds, much green food.

**Behavior:** Peacable and quiet. Pairs are closely bonded.

**Remarks:** Abundant species. Regular breeding. Guard against worm infestations.

**Scientific Name:** *Psephotus chrysopterygius dissimilis*

**Habitat:** Dry forest and savanna regions. Northern Australia.

**Characteristics:** Subspecies of the golden-shouldered parakeet. L 10 in (26 cm). M upper side brownish gray, underside and rump turquoise. Top of head to nape blackish brown. Lower belly and undertail coverts bright red. Wing coverts golden yellow. F duller; breast and front of neck yellowish green.

**Life in the Wild:** Nests in termite hills, more rarely in tree hollows; 4–6 eggs, B 20 days, N 35 days, V–I.

**Care:** Aviary with protected room. Provide for food seeking on the ground.

**Feeding:** Various seeds, especially sprouted and half-ripe ones; soft food.

**Behavior:** Aggressive. Keep only one pair.

**Remarks:** Not endangered but a rather rare species. Since the termite hills store heat, the F protects the young too little. Therefore, the brooding enclosure must be temperate.

**Scientific Name:**
*Purpureicephalus spurius*
**Habitat:** Eucalyptus forests, parks, orchards. Southwestern Australia.
**Characteristics:** L 14½ in (37 cm). M upper side green, breast and belly lavender blue. Top of head, sides, thighs, and undertail coverts red. F duller, red-greenish tinged. The long, narrow beak facilitates removal of the eucalyptus kernel.
**Life in the Wild:** Brooding hollows at great heights; 3–7 eggs, B 20 days, N 35 days, X–XII. Feeds on eucalyptus seeds, nectar, buds, grass awns, insects. Plunders orchards. Abundant despite extermination.
**Care:** Aviary 16½ ft (5 m) in length; unheated shelter area. Gnaws wooden constructions. Provide shallow bathing dishes.
**Feeding:** Mixed grains for large parrots, peanuts, half-ripe wheat, corncobs, much fruit and green food.
**Behavior:** Gets along with smaller parakeet species. Voice not very loud. Remains shy.
**Remarks:** Abundant species. Breeding often successful.

# Pale-headed Rosella

**Scientific Name:** *Platycercus adscitus*

**Habitat:** Eucalyptus savannas. Queensland and New South Wales (Australia).

**Characteristics:** L 12 in (30 cm). M and F head yellow-white, back feathers black with yellow edges. Lower back, breast, and belly blue. Under-tail coverts red. F with white spot on underside of wing. 2 SS.

**Life in the Wild:** Nests at great heights in deep tree hollows; 3–8 eggs, B 20 days, N 32 days, XI–IV. Feeds on grass and eucalyptus seeds, half-ripe corn, fruit, and insects.

**Care:** Keep in pairs in aviary approximately 16½ ft (5 m) long with frost-free shelter. House away from other rosella species and broad-tailed para-keets.

**Feeding:** Millet, canary grass seed, sunflower seeds, thistle seeds, fresh corncobs, apples, carrots, green food.

**Behavior:** Incompatible with other birds. Loud voice.

**Remarks:** Easy to breed in aviary. A tree trunk is recommended for nesting place.

**Scientific Name:** *Platycercus icterotis*

**Habitat:** Open country. Southwestern Australia.

**Characteristics:** L 10 in (25 cm). M head and underside red, yellow cheek spots. Feathers of upper back and shoulders black with green edges, wing coverts blue. F with paler, smaller cheek spot. Head and upper breast green, red band on forehead. Belly pale red with some green. 2 SS.

**Life in the Wild:** Nests in tree hollows; 6–8 eggs, B 20 days, N 33 days, VIII–XII. Follows civilization. Clearing of woods promotes spread.

**Care:** Aviary at least 6½ ft (2 m) long; frost-free protected area. Flat bathing dishes.

**Feeding:** Grain mixtures for large parrots, weed seeds, carrots, apples, berries, green food.

**Behavior:** Always in motion. Tame; gets along well with other species. Does not gnaw. Tolerable voice. Pairs stay together all year round.

**Remarks:** Abundant species. Especially recommended for beginners. Easy to breed.

**Scientific Name:** *Platycercus eximius*

**Habitat:** Savannas, gardens, and parks. Southeastern Australia, Tasmania; introduced into New Zealand.

**Characteristics:** L 12½ in (32 cm). M head, neck, breast, and undertail coverts red. White cheek spot. Feathers of back and tail black with yellow edges. F paler; cheek spot dirty white. 3 SS.

**Life in the Wild:** Usually two broods. Nests in tree hollows and in rabbit burrows; 5–7 eggs, B 20 days, N 33 days, IX–I. Feeds on grass and weed seeds, wheat kernels. Follows civilization. Larvae of a moth species live in the nests and eat the feces of the young.

**Care:** Keep in pairs. Aviary at least 13 ft (4 m) long. Provide bathing facilities. Tolerates frost.

**Feeding:** Grains for large parrots, apples, carrots, green food.

**Behavior:** Loud voice. Aggressive toward other birds.

**Remarks:** Abundant species. Easy to breed.

**Scientific Name:** *Platycercus elegans elegans*

**Habitat:** Forests. Southeastern Australia; introduced into New Zealand and Norfolk islands.

**Characteristics:** L 14 in (36 cm). M and F head and body glowing red. Blue cheek spot. Feathers of upper back and shoulders black with red edges, tail blue. Juvenile plumage green, red in northern SS. 3 SS.

**Life in the Wild:** Nests in large treetop hollows; 5–8 eggs, B 20 days, N 35 days, VIII–II. Feeds on grass and other seeds, insect larvae. Local disappearance as a result of clearing.

**Care:** Aviary at least 13 ft (4 m) long. Unheated protected area. Facilities for bathing.

**Feeding:** Grain mixture for large parrots, corn, carrots, apples, green food.

**Behavior:** Powerful need to gnaw. Utters melodious sounds. Courting M puffs up breast plumage, shakes spread tail.

**Remarks:** Abundant species. Breeding not difficult. Deep natural hollows required.

**Scientific Name:** *Nymphicus hollandicus*

**Habitat:** Cleared countryside. Central Australia.

**Characteristics:** L 12½ in (32 cm). Gray. M forehead, cheeks, crest, and throat yellow; ear region red-brown. F head and crest gray, a little yellow. Underside of tail striped horizontally with gray and yellow. Feathered crest indicates possible relationship with cockatoos. Mutations. As among cockatoos, M broods also.

**Life in the Wild:** Nests in tree hollows at lesser heights; 4–7 eggs, B 20 days, N 30 days, VIII–XII. Several broods possible. Seeks food on the ground. Nomadic.

**Care:** Aviary at least 6½ ft (2 m) long. Keep tame animals in a room cage; daily free flight.

**Feeding:** Grain mixtures for medium parrots with a few sunflower seed kernels, millet spray, apples, carrots, green food.

**Behavior:** Sociable. When disturbed while nesting hisses threateningly, with sideways swinging of body. Gnaws little.

**Remarks:** Abundant species.

# Australian King Parakeet

**Scientific Name:** *Alisterus scapularis*

**Habitat:** Damp coastal forests. Southeastern Australia.

**Characteristics:** L 17 in (43 cm). M back and wings dark green; head, neck, and underside red. Dark blue rump and neckband. Red beak. F green. Red belly, blue rump, black beak. 2 SS.

**Life in the Wild:** Nests in hollow forest trees; 3–6 eggs, B 21 days, N about 45 days, IX–I. Lives in pairs, family groups, small groups of young birds with immature plumage. Feeds on berries, fruits, buds, seeds, grain, and corn. Local disappearance as a result of clearing.

**Care:** Aviary with sheltered area. Can tolerate cold.

**Feeding:** Grain mixture for large parrots, wheat, oats, peanuts, fresh corncobs, apples, carrots, green food.

**Behavior:** Gets along with other species. Does not gnaw. Courting M ruffles head feathers with wings folded back.

**Remarks:** Difficult to breed. M may torment F. Life expectancy about 30 years.

# Crimson-winged Parakeet

**Scientific Name:** *Aprosmictus erythropterus erythropterus*
**Habitat:** Thin forests. Northeastern Australia and southern New Guinea.
**Characteristics:** L 13 in (33 cm). M green, upper back and shoulders black, wing coverts red, red beak. F duller, no black, less red, brownish beak. 3 SS.
**Life in the Wild:** Nests in eucalyptus tree hollows up to 29½ ft (9 m) deep; 3–6 eggs, B 21 days, N 40 days, IX–XII. Lives in pairs, in small groups after brooding; also joins with king parakeets, mealy rosellas, and Barnard's parakeets.
**Care:** Aviary at least 13 ft (4 m) long with protected area. Facilities for bathing. Keep only one pair per enclosure. In the spring M harries F. Clipping several primaries of the M lessens the danger to the F.
**Feeding:** Grain mixture for large parrots, wheat, oats, peanuts, fresh corncobs, apples, carrots, green food.
**Behavior:** Only young birds are compatible with other species.
**Remarks:** Abundant species.

# Princess of Wales Parrot

**Scientific Name:** *Polytelis alexandrae*

**Habitat:** Dry prairies with scattered trees on stream banks. Western Australia.

**Characteristics:** L 17½ in (45 cm). M back olive green, belly gray-green, rump violet-blue, blue crown. Chin, throat, cheeks, and thighs pink. Very long tail feathers. F head blue-gray, paler. Mutations.

**Life in the Wild:** Broods in colonies; up to 10 pairs in 1 tree; 4–6 eggs, B 19 days, N 35 days, IX–I. Nomadic and obscure way of life. Feeds mainly on porcupine grass seeds.

**Care:** Long aviary with protected area secure against frost.

**Feeding:** Grain mixture for large parrots, pine nuts, peanuts, oats, wheat, fresh corncobs, apples, carrots, much green food.

**Behavior:** Gets along with own species and others. M undertakes courtship flights.

**Remarks:** Not endangered but a rather rare species. Breeding is possible. Thick branches needed for roosting.

# Barraband's Parakeet

**Scientific Name:** *Polytelis swainsonii*

**Habitat:** Damp savannas and woods. New South Wales, Victoria (Australia).

**Characteristics:** L 15½ in (40 cm). M green. Forehead, chin, and throat yellow; lower throat with crescent-shaped red scutum. F without yellow and red, paler.

**Life in the Wild:** Nests in high branch hollows; 4–6 eggs, B 19 days, N 35 days, IX–XII. Feeds mainly on seeds, grain, berries, and flower nectar. M in small groups until brooding time.

**Care:** Aviary at least 16 ft (5 m) long. Dry, draft-free interior room necessary. Heating not required. Enjoys bathing in the rain or under a spray.

**Feeding:** Grain mixture for large parrots with addition of a small amount of fatty seeds, fruit, berries (elder, mountain ash).

**Behavior:** Becomes tame. Gets along with own species in a large aviary. Loud cries during courtship.

**Remarks:** Abundant species. Breeding is possible.

**Scientific Name:** *Eclectus roratus*

**Habitat:** Rain forest. New Guinea and offshore islands, northeastern Australia.

**Characteristics:** L 15 in (38 cm). M green. Head and neck yellowish, sides of body and undersides of wings red. F head and back red, underside bluish red. Hairlike feather structure. 10 SS.

**Life in the Wild:** Broods in tree hollows several feet deep with entry over 65½ ft (20 m) high; 2–3 eggs, B 28 days, N 75 days.

**Care:** Room cage of at least 1 cu yd (1 m³) or aviary 13 ft (4 m) long with heatable inner enclosure. Do not keep at under 59° F (15° C). Gnaws very little.

**Feeding:** Sunflower seed kernels, millet, canary grass seed, peanuts, pine nuts, millet spray, sweet fruit, haws or hips, fresh corncobs, green peas, carrots, celery, tomatoes, green food.

**Behavior:** F more dominant than M, often aggressive.

**Remarks:** Breeding often successful even in a room cage. High vitamin A requirement.

**Scientific Name:** *Psittacula eupatria*
**Habitat:** Forests, cultivated land, parks. Pakistan, India to Vietnam, Sri Lanka.
**Characteristics:** L 23 in (58 cm). Green. M with black neck band, pink band on nape, red-brown shoulder spot. F without marking bands, shoulder spot paler. 6 SS. Mutations.
**Life in the Wild:** Nests in tree hollows, chimneys, holes in walls; 2–4 eggs, B 28 days, N 45 days, XI–IV. Often several pairs in one tree. Thousands roost in trees in the evening.

**Care:** Metal aviary 13 ft (4 m) long; large parrot cage and supervised free flight in room. Sensitive to frost.
**Feeding:** Sunflower seed kernels, hemp, corn, wheat, peanuts, pine nuts, fruit, greens.
**Behavior:** Pairs stay together only during brooding time. F dominates in rank. Intelligent (like large parrot species).
**Remarks:** Abundant species. Breeding possible. F spends night in nest box. The first parrot species to be imported to Europe (at time of Alexander the Great).

**Scientific Name:** *Psittacula krameri*

**Habitat:** Damp forests, cultivated land, and cities. Western and central Africa, Pakistan, Nepal, Burma, India, Sri Lanka.

**Characteristics:** L 16½ in (42 cm). Green. M with black neck band, pink band on nape, and black stripe between nostrils and eyes. 6 SS. Mutations.

**Life in the Wild:** Takes advantage of every opportunity (especially in Asia) to obtain food and to brood; 3–6 eggs, B 23 days, N 45 days; XII–VI (Asiatic SS), rainy season (African SS).

**Care:** Possible to keep colonies. Tolerates light frost; nevertheless provide temperate protected area.

**Feeding:** Primarily nonfatty seeds, fruit.

**Behavior:** Flocks in roosting places. Likes to bathe in the rain. No firm pair bonding. F dominates.

**Remarks:** Abundant species. Easy to breed. Most widely distributed parrot species.

**Scientific Name:** *Psittacula alexandri*

**Habitat:** Laurel and bamboo woods. Northern India, Nepal, Burma, southern China, Indochina to Java and Bali.

**Characteristics:** L 15½ in (40 cm). M and F green. Head gray, black forehead stripe, black stripe under the cheeks. Crop and breast pink. M upper beak red, F black. 7 SS.

**Life in the Wild:** Several pairs brood in one tree; 3–4 eggs, B 22 days, N 45 days, XII–IV. Small groups in rice and wheat fields. Swarms of over 10,000 at feeding places.

**Care:** Aviary of metal 10 ft (3 m) long with protected area. Offer feed and water on a high table. Fresh branches for gnawing. Sleeping holes.

**Feeding:** Grains for large parrots, pine nuts, apples.

**Behavior:** M provides F with food, and F feeds young. During courtship M sits beside F and trills while making turning movements with head.

**Remarks:** Abundant species. To date only few bred in captivity.

**Scientific Name:** *Psittacula derbyana*

**Habitat:** Mountain forests, mountain country up to 11,500 ft (3500 m). Tibet, Assam, southwestern China.

**Characteristics:** L 19½ in (50 cm). M and F green. Underside bluish green, forehead and cheeks blue. Lower cheek edged with black stripe. M upper beak red, F black.

**Life in the Wild:** Nests in tree hollows; 2–4 eggs, B 27 days, N 49 days, VI. Groups of up to 50 birds in fields.

Northernmost parrot species.

**Care:** Aviary cage of metal at least 13 ft (4 m) in length. Being a mountain dweller, not sensitive to cold. Nest boxes used for roosting all year long. Enjoys fresh branches.

**Feeding:** Grain mixtures for large parrots, peanuts, fruit.

**Behavior:** Courting M struts with legs raised very high and fanned tail feathers. Pupils contract. F can feed M.

**Remarks:** Abundant species. To date only few bred.

# Plum-headed Parakeet

**Scientific Name:** *Psittacula cyanocephala*

**Habitat:** Forests at elevations up to 4200 ft (1300 m) in the vicinity of cultivated plains. India, western Pakistan, Nepal.

**Characteristics:** L 13½ in (35 cm). M green, plum-colored head, black neck ring, blue-green band on nape, brown-red shoulder spot. F without shoulder spot, head blue-gray. Plumage fully colored only after 2 years.

**Life in the Wild:** Nests in tree hollows (often several pairs in one tree) or holes in walls; 4–5 eggs, B 23 days, N 49 days, XII–IV. Swarms in orchards and wheat fields. Community roosting places.

**Care:** Aviary at least 6½ ft (2 m) long, frost-free protected area. Gnaws very little. Nest boxes used all year long as sleeping holes.

**Feeding:** Grain mixtures for large parrots, fruit, green food.

**Behavior:** Tolerable voice. Also gets along with small birds. M begins to court in late winter; sings and runs back and forth in front of F.

**Remarks:** Abundant species.

**Scientific Name:** *Agapornis roseicollis*

**Habitat:** Prairies and savannas up to 5200 ft (1600 m). Namibia, southwestern Angola.

**Characteristics:** L 6 in (16 cm). M and F green, face region pink, rump blue. 2 SS. Many mutations.

**Life in the Wild:** Nests in colonies in holes, under hut roofs, in empty bird nests; 4–5 eggs, B 23 days, N 40 days, I–III. Flocks in grain fields.

**Care:** Pairs in strong cages at least 27½ in (70 cm) long. Garden aviaries with protected areas. Sleeping boxes, fresh willow branches as nesting material. Shallow bathing dishes.

**Feeding:** Commercially available grain feed, fruit, green food, millet spray.

**Behavior:** Very close pair bonding ("lovebirds"). Aggressive toward other bird species. F carries in nesting material in back feathers.

**Remarks:** Numerous species. Easily bred. Dry room air produces hatching problems.

**Scientific Name:** *Agapornis personata*

**Habitat:** Grassy prairies with some trees. Northeastern Tanzania; introduced into Kenya.

**Characteristics:** L 6 in (15 cm). M and F green, head almost black, yellow breast, white eye ring. Mutations.

**Life in the Wild:** Broods in colonies in branch hollows, abandoned bird nests, and niches in walls; 4–6 eggs, B 22 days, N 40 days, III–VIII. Food consists primarily of grass awns. Visits corn and millet fields.

**Care:** Keep in pairs. Cage with sleeping box and shallow bathing dishes. Free flight in the house under supervision. Aviary with frost-free protected area. Fresh branches are gnawed down and carried in as building material.

**Feeding:** Commercial grain mixtures, fruit, green food, protein-rich brooding feed.

**Behavior:** Intolerant of other bird species, sometimes also of own species.

**Remarks:** When free sometimes interbreeds with Fischer's lovebird.

**Scientific Name:** *Agapornis fischeri*

**Habitat:** Savannas with trees. Northern Tanzania.

**Characteristics:** L 6 in (15 cm). M and F green. Forehead and face orange, back of head brownish, breast yellowish. Yellow and blue mutations.

**Life in the Wild:** Nests in tree hollows, woven nests, on buildings; 4–6 eggs, B 22 days, N 40 days, V–VII. At wheat-ripening time flocks to the fields.

**Care:** Cage at least 27½ in (70 cm) long with strong mesh. Only in pairs; in aviary several pairs. Sensitive to frost. Nest boxes used all year long as roosting places. Fresh branches, bathing dishes.

**Feeding:** Commercial grain mixtures, fruit, green food.

**Behavior:** Compatible with black-cheeked lovebird but not with other bird species. F builds a roofed nest.

**Remarks:** Abundant species; is also exterminated. Breeding succeeds easily. Do not cross with other species. Is often alleged to be SS of black-cheeked lovebird.

# Madagascar Lovebird

**Scientific Name:** *Agapornis cana*

**Habitat:** Bush country with light stands of bamboo. Madagascar; also introduced into adjacent islands.

**Characteristics:** L 5 in (13 cm). M upper side dark green, underside yellowish green, breast and head pale gray. F green. 2 SS.

**Life in the Wild:** Broods in tree hollows; 5–7 eggs, B 22 days, N 45 days, XI–XII. Searches for food on the ground and in rice fields.

**Care:** Only in pairs, since F is quarrelsome. Large budgerigar cage or outdoor aviary with protected area. Temperature not under 50° F (10° C). Nest boxes used all year as roosting places. Branches with leaves for nesting material.

**Feeding:** Small seeds, niger seed, thistle seed, small sunflower seeds, millet sprays.

**Behavior:** Shyer than the other lovebirds. F transports nesting materials in back and breast feathers.

**Remarks:** Export forbidden. Declining due to loss of habitat. Captive breeding urgent.

# African Gray Parrot

**Scientific Name:** *Psittacus erithacus*

**Habitat:** Forests. Equatorial Africa from the Ivory Coast to northwestern Tanzania.

**Characteristics:** L 14 in (36 cm). M and F gray. Face region unfeathered, tail feathers red. 3 SS.

**Life in the Wild:** Breeds in tree hollows; 3–4 eggs, B 29 days, N 80 days. Lives in large flocks after brooding period. Seeks food in grain fields.

**Care:** Needs long time for acclimation and to become tame. Large cage. Free flight under supervision. Lukewarm showers, much occupation. Garden aviary with heatable protected area in a somewhat shady location.

**Feeding:** Commercially available feed grains.

**Behavior:** Very intelligent. Best imitator among the parrots. Boredom and changes of environment often result in feather plucking.

**Remarks:** Still plentiful in nature. Young birds (gray iris) become tame quickly. Breeding is often successful.

# Senegal Parrot

**Scientific Name:**
*Poicephalus senegalus*

**Habitat:** Thin forests in central Africa.

**Characteristics:** L 9½ in (24 cm). M and F green. Head gray, breast and belly yellow to orange. Juvenile birds recognizable by darker or grayer iris. 3 SS.

**Life in the Wild:** Broods in tree hollows; 2–4 eggs, B 27 days, N 75 days. Pairs or small groups. Gathers food in trees (buds, fruit, especially figs) and in grain fields.

**Care:** Large parrot cage. Juvenile birds become very tame and are suitable for keeping indoors—with regular free flight. Otherwise keep in an aviary at least 13 ft (4 m) long with protected area; minimum temperature 50° F (10° C).

**Feeding:** Sunflower seed kernels, small seeds, wheat, oats, fresh corncobs, apples, carrots.

**Behavior:** Close pair bonding. Not a very loud voice.

**Remarks:** Abundant species. May live to be more than 40 years of age.

**Scientific Name:** *Amazona ochrocephala*

**Habitat:** Dry forest regions, savannas. Mouth of Amazon to Mexico.

**Characteristics:** L 14 in (36 cm). M and F green. Front edge of wing red, head region yellow. 8 SS.

**Life in the Wild:** Broods in tree hollows; 2–3 eggs, B 26 days, N 75 days, XII/I (south), V/VI (north). Some SS follow civilization.

**Care:** Very popular as a ''talker.'' Single birds need much contact with their caretakers. Large, strong cage. Keep free on a parrot stand. Keeping in pairs in an outdoor aviary is best. Heatable protected space, facilities for bathing (spray).

**Feeding:** Sunflower seed kernels, corn, wheat, oats, peanuts, pine nuts, fruit, green food; also sprouted or half-ripe grain.

**Behavior:** Close pair bonding, probably lifelong monogamy.

**Remarks:** Still abundant but declining in some areas. Breeding repeatedly successful.

# Orange-winged Amazon

**Scientific Name:** *Amazona amazonica*
**Habitat:** Humid regions. Northern half of South America.
**Characteristics:** L 12½ in (32 cm). M and F green. Forehead and crown blue, cheeks and edges of wings yellow. Orange-red wing speculum, 4 outermost tail feathers red underneath. 2–3 SS.
**Life in the Wild:** Broods in tree hollows over 5 ft (1½ m) deep; 2–5 eggs, B 26 days, N 80 days, II–VIII. Flocks in roosting trees. Seeks food primarily in trees.

**Care:** Keeping single birds possible only with close contact with caretaker; left alone, tame birds scream (attempts at contact). Climbing and bathing facilities. Temperature not under 50° F (10° C).
**Feeding:** Grain mixtures for parrots, fresh corncobs, fruit.
**Behavior:** Very adept climber, waddling gait. Caged birds almost give up flying.
**Remarks:** Breeding possible but takes time. Commonest and most widely distributed amazon.

# Blue-fronted Amazon

**Scientific Name:** *Amazona aestiva aestiva*
**Habitat:** Tropical forest, bush country. Central Brazil.
**Characteristics:** L 13½ to 16 in (35–41 cm). M and F green. Forehead and bridle blue, face and throat yellow, tops and wing edges red. Coloring can vary greatly. 2 SS.
**Life in the Wild:** Broods in tree hollows; 2–5 eggs, B 26 days, N 65 days, X–III. Large flocks after brooding period. Nomadic.
**Care:** Single bird may be kept only when "family bonding" is complete. Aviary with climbing branches, heatable protected area. Spray during warm weather.
**Feeding:** Grain mixtures for parrots, fresh corncobs, half-ripe wheat, fruit.
**Behavior:** Close pair bonding. Feeding during courtship. Introduces nesting materials. Capability of imitation varies.
**Remarks:** Still numerous in spite of partial destruction of native habitat. Breeding of tame birds has been successful a number of times. Ready to breed at 5 years.

# Spectacled Parrotlet

**Scientific Name:** *Forpus conspicillatus*

**Habitat:** Open forest regions and savannas up to 5200 ft (1600 m). Eastern Panama, western Venezuela, Colombia.

**Characteristics:** L 4½ in (12 cm). Green. M has blue rump, secondaries, primary coverts, and eye ring. 3 SS.

**Life in the Wild:** Nests in tree hollows; 4–6 eggs, B 21 days, N 32 days, I–III. After brooding period seeks food in flocks (berries, fruit, grass awns, half-ripe rice).

**Care:** Pairs. Large budgerigar cage or aviary. Sensitive to frost. Establish feeding places high in cage. Do not bathe.

**Feeding:** Small seeds, sunflower kernels, millet spray (all also sprouted); corncobs, fruit, carrots.

**Behavior:** Close pair bonding. Gets along with smaller birds in an aviary. Young feed independently almost immediately after they leave the nest.

**Remarks:** Numerous in native habitat but scarcely imported anymore. Development of breeding stock important.

# Blue-headed or Red-vented Parrot

**Scientific Name:** *Pionus menstruus*

**Habitat:** Forests in vicinity of streams. Southern Costa Rica to northern Bolivia and Brazil.

**Characteristics:** L 11 in (28 cm). M and F green. Head, neck, and breast blue. (Throat in *P. m. rubrigularis* somewhat pink.) Cheeks black, rump red. 3 SS.

**Life in the Wild:** Broods in tree hollows; 3–5 eggs, B 28 days, N 70 days, II–IV. Travels to the food supply.

**Care:** Strong, large parrot cage. Climbing facilities, fresh branches for gnawing. Aviary with protected area; temperature not under 50° F (10° C).

**Feeding:** Sunflower, canary grass, and other small seeds, pine nuts, corncobs, carrots, much fruit, green food.

**Behavior:** Gets along with members of own species. Not a screamer. Gnaws on cage beams a bit. Juveniles become very tame, are gentler than amazons.

**Remarks:** Abundant in the wild. Breeding frequently successful; young must often be hand-raised.

# Canary-winged Parakeet

**Scientific Name:** *Brotogeris versicolorus chiriri*
**Habitat:** Forest regions. Brazil, Bolivia, Paraguay, northern Argentina.
**Characteristics:** L 8½ in (22 cm). M and F green. Pinions black, blue, and white; secondaries yellow. 3 SS.
**Life in the Wild:** Nests in tree hollows, nests of tree termites; 5–6 eggs, B 23 days, N 50 days, IV–VI. Very slow juvenile development. Common roosting trees.
**Care:** Keep only in pairs until brooding time. Protect from frost. Facilities for climbing and bathing.
**Feeding:** Mixed grain for large parrots, much fruit and green food.
**Behavior:** Close pair bonding. Loud, screeching cries. When threatened raises the wings from the body and claps them together with an explosive sound.
**Remarks:** Abundant species. To date has seldom been bred. Even after the first flight the young still sleep in the nest for some time.

**Scientific Name:**
*Bolborhynchus lineola*
**Habitat:** Mountain forests. Southern Mexico to Peru.
**Characteristics:** L 6½ in (17 cm). M and F green with yellowish underside. Black horizontal striping on sides and on top.
**Life in the Wild:** Nests in tree hollows; 3–6 eggs, B 19 days, N 38 days. Small groups; after the brooding period flocks of over 100. Well camouflaged.
**Care:** Nesting boxes are used all year round as roosting places. Sensitive to frost. Shaded spots—aviaries can be planted—are favorite resting places. Needs strong branches to walk along.
**Feeding:** Gladly eats millet spray and panicles, sunflower seed kernels, apples stuck on branches, carrots, green food.
**Behavior:** With body balanced can slide along branches. Social preening rare.
**Remarks:** Good success in breeding with birds kept in colonies. Claws grow very quickly; shortening required.

**Scientific Name:** *Myiopsitta monachus*

**Habitat:** Sparse woods, bush and farm land. Bolivia, Brazil, Argentina.

**Characteristics:** L 12 in (30 cm). M and F green. Forehead, face, neck, and breast gray. Blue and yellow mutations. 2 SS.

**Life in the Wild:** The only parrot species with a free-standing community nest; 5–8 eggs, B 26 days, N 42 days, X. Follows civilization; causes great damage to fields.

**Care:** In the aviary builds a gigantic nest, for which branches about 20 in (½ m) long should be provided daily. The nest provides sufficient protection against low temperatures. Brooding also takes place in nest boxes.

**Feeding:** Mixed grain for large parrots, fruit, carrots, green food.

**Behavior:** Loud voice. Close pair bonding. After the brooding period symbolic feeding of partner serves as a sign of belonging together.

**Remarks:** Can be maintained flying free. Damages garden.

**Scientific Name:** *Pyrrhura frontalis*
**Habitat:** Primarily forests. Brazil, Uruguay, Paraguay, northern Argentina.
**Characteristics:** L 10 in (26 cm). M and F green. Olive neck, throat, and breast; yellow-edged feathers. Dark red spot on belly. Ear region gray-brown. 3 SS.
**Life in the Wild:** Broods in tree hollows; 3–6 eggs, B 27 days, N 50 days. In company with other parrots seeks blooming trees and fields with ripening wheat; insects and larvae provide additional food.
**Care:** Aviary at least 6½ ft (2 m) long. Possible to keep a colony. Nest boxes are used all year long as roosting places. Facilities for bathing required. Fresh branches.
**Feeding:** Feed grain for large parrots, apples, much green food, fresh corncobs.
**Behavior:** M defends nest; otherwise agreeable, even with other species. Several pairs will spend the night together in one nest.
**Remarks:** Breeding not difficult. Often two broods per year.

**Scientific Name:** *Aratinga jandaya*

**Habitat:** Forest clearings, coconut palm groves. North-eastern Brazil.

**Characteristics:** L 12 in (30 cm). M and F head, neck, and upper breast brilliant yellow. Underside and lower back orange-red, pinions and tail tip blue, otherwise green. Dirty white eye ring.

**Life in the Wild:** Nests in tree hollows; 3–4 eggs, B 26 days, N 55 days, IX–X.

**Care:** Aviary at least 10 ft (3 m) long with protected area; any wooden constructions will be destroyed. Bathing facilities required. Provide many fresh branches.

**Feeding:** Grain mixture for large parrots, fruit, carrots, green food. Fresh corn is a popular brooding food.

**Behavior:** Loud voice functions to ensure that the flock stays together. Gets along with own species and with other bird species.

**Remarks:** Breeding also possible when colonies are kept. Two broods per year.

**Scientific Name:** *Aratinga guarouba*

**Habitat:** Tropical rain forests. Northeastern Brazil.

**Characteristics:** L 15 in (38 cm). M and F golden yellow with green primaries and secondaries.

**Life in the Wild:** Nests in tree hollows; 2–3 eggs, B 29 days, N 65 days, X. Seeks food mainly in treetops. Declining because of destruction of habitat.

**Care:** Aviary of metal. Temperate protected area, high humidity. Facilities for bathing.

**Feeding:** Large parrot mixture, half-ripe wheat, peanuts, berries, apples, green food.

**Behavior:** Very close pair bonding. During courtship feeding one wing is laid over the partner. Gets along with own species; other species will be attacked. Loud voice. Outstandingly playful behavior.

**Remarks:** Endangered species, entered on first list of the international endangered species agreement. Thus only animals bred in captivity are available.

# Sun Conure

**Scientific Name:** *Aratinga solstitialis*

**Habitat:** Savannas and thin woods. Guyana, Venezuela, northern Brazil.

**Characteristics:** L 12 in (30 cm). M and F orange-yellow. Forehead, cheeks, belly, and lower back orange-red. Yellow wings; secondaries partly green.

**Life in the Wild:** Nests in tree hollows; 3–6 eggs, B 27 days, N 50 days, II. Large flocks search for food in trees.

**Care:** Aviary with frost-free protected area. Wooden boards will be badly gnawed. Bathing facilities and fresh branches necessary. Keep imported birds at about 68° F (20° C) at first.

**Feeding:** Grain mixture for large parrots, especially sunflower seed kernels and canary grass seed; apples, green food.

**Behavior:** Loud voice. Close pair bonding; social preening. Single birds bond very closely to their caretaker.

**Remarks:** Abundant species. Breeding possible. Not unusual to have 2–3 broods per year.

**Scientific Name:** *Aratinga aurea*

**Habitat:** Open country. Brazil, Bolivia, Paraguay, northwestern Argentina.

**Characteristics:** L 11 in (28 cm). M and F green. Forehead spot orange-yellow, crown and bridle blue, neck and breast olive brown. 2 SS.

**Life in the Wild:** Nests in tree hollows; 2–6 eggs, B 26 days, N 50 days. Searches for food in trees and on the ground; also consumes insects. Widening of habitat as a result of land clearing.

**Care:** Aviary of at least 6½ ft (2 m) in length; wooden construction will be gnawed only slightly. Bathing facilities and roosting boxes required.

**Feeding:** Grain mixtures for large parrots, apples.

**Behavior:** Loud voice. Tolerates other species only outside the brooding period. Defends nest even against caretaker. From the 4th week care of young by M only.

**Remarks:** Abundant species. Easy to breed. Single animals become tame. Life expectancy more than 20 years.

# Patagonian Conure

**Scientific Name:**
*Cyanoliseus patagonus*
**Habitat:** Forests and grassy plains devoid of trees. Argentina, Chile.
**Characteristics:** L 17–21 in (43–53 cm), depending on SS. M and F olive-brown. Forehead black-brown, upper breast whitish, belly yellow with red center, red thigh. 3 SS.
**Life in the Wild:** Broods in colonies in clay and sandstone walls; brooding holes with entrance passages up to 10 ft (3 m) long; 2–3 eggs, B 25 days, N 60 days, IX–XII.

Declining mainly because of extermination.
**Care:** Aviary of metal. Not very sensitive to cold and dampness. Bathing facilities; fresh branches.
**Feeding:** Sunflower seed kernels, oats, millet, corn, polished seeds, peanuts, apples, carrots, green food.
**Behavior:** Loud voice. Gets along with own species, not with other species. Need to gnaw is very strong.
**Remarks:** Breeding is possible. Offer a strong natural trunk of hardwood for nesting.

**Scientific Name:** *Ara macao*
**Habitat:** Low-lying humid areas. Southern Mexico, Central America, central and northern South America.
**Characteristics:** L 33½ in (85 cm). M and F brilliant red. Primaries and tail coverts blue, greater wing coverts and shoulder coverts yellow, undersides of wings red-brown. Lower back and rump light blue. Cheek region bare and white with red feather lines.
**Life in the Wild:** Broods in tree hollows; 2–4 eggs, B 26 days, N 90 days, XI–IV. Flies up to 18½ mi (30 km) to feed on palm fruit, figs, mangoes, and beetle larvae.
**Care:** Room aviaries, parrot stands. Aviary not under 19½ ft (6 m) in length, if possible, with heatable interior room. Constant supply of fresh branches for occupation.
**Feeding:** Sunflower seed kernels, pine nuts, peanuts, walnuts, corn (especially fresh cobs), much fruit.
**Behavior:** Probably lifelong monogamy.
**Remarks:** Endangered species. Breeding possible.

**Scientific Name:**
*Ara chloroptera*
**Habitat:** Tropical virgin forest. Southeastern Panama, central and northern South America.
**Characteristics:** L 35½ in (90 cm). M and F dark red. Median and greater wing coverts green, most of the flight feathers blue, undersides of wings red-brown. Light blue rump and upper and lower tail coverts. Bare whitish face area with red feather lines.
**Life in the Wild:** Nests in tree hollows and broken palm trunks; 2–3 eggs, B 28 days, N 95 days; XI/XII (south), II/III (north). Pairs or family groups.
**Care:** Becomes tame quickly. Large, strong cage and parrot stand as a free perch when kept in the house. Aviary in the garden with heatable interior room. Provide fresh branches.
**Feeding:** Sunflower seed kernels, various nuts, fresh corn, fruit.
**Behavior:** Quiet, very intelligent species. Close pair bonding.
**Remarks:** Breeding has been successful a number of times. Diminishing sporadically.

**Scientific Name:** *Ara severa*
**Habitat:** Forests along rivers. Panama to northern Bolivia, northern Brazil.
**Characteristics:** L 19 in (48 cm). M and F green. Crown bluish, forehead black-brown. Front edge of wing red. Naked cheek with black feather lines. 2 SS.
**Life in the Wild:** Broods in tree hollows; 2–5 eggs, B 26 days, N 70 days, XI–III.
**Care:** Usually does not become as tame as the larger species. If possible keep in pairs. Room or garden aviary with heatable protected area. Provide many fresh branches.
**Feeding:** Commercially available parrot feed, canary grass seed, millet, fresh corncobs, hips or haws (deep-frozen supply), carrots, green food, much fruit.
**Behavior:** Close pair bonding. Much livelier than the somewhat cumbersome large macaws.
**Remarks:** Generally abundant species. Destruction of habitat and extermination for fruit culture produce local declines. Breeding possible.

**Scientific Name:**
*Ara ararauna*
**Habitat:** Mangrove forests, tropical forests, savannas. Eastern Panama, central and northern South America.
**Characteristics:** L 35½ in (90 cm). M and F blue. Underside yellow, forehead green, throat black. Bare cheek region with black feather lines.
**Life in the Wild:** Nests in tree hollows; 2–4 eggs, B 27 days, N 90 days, XI–V. Seeks food in small groups. Over 100 animals may congregate in roosting trees.

**Care:** Room cages of strong mesh, climbing branches. Aviaries with heatable protected area. Fresh branches, pinecones, stones, etc. as playthings.
**Feeding:** Commercially available parrot feed, much fruit, mealworms, cheese.
**Behavior:** Close pair bonding, therefore also close attachment to caretaker by single animals. Very active and interested.
**Remarks:** Declining in some areas; overall still not endangered. Breeding repeatedly successful.

**Scientific Name:**
*Anodorhynchus hyacinthinus*
**Habitat:** Palm forests, dry savannas. Highlands in central and southern Brazil.
**Characteristics:** L up to 39½ in (100 cm); largest parrot species. M and F cobalt blue. Bare skin at base of lower mandible and eye ring orange-yellow.
**Life in the Wild:** Nests in palm trunks, holes in rocks; 2–3 eggs, B 28 days, N 100 days. Feeds on palm nuts, fruit, and snails among other things.
**Care:** Particularly strong cage or aviary; climbing tree if kept in the house. Keeping on a chain or on a ring is to be avoided.
**Feeding:** Primarily pine nuts, peanuts, and other nuts; also sunflower seed kernels, corn ears, and fruit, occasionally a bone and cooked meat.
**Behavior:** Especially close pair bonding, yet never snappish with trusted people.
**Remarks:** Declining sporadically. Further import hardly possible anymore. Breeding of animals in captivity is urgent.

### Identifying Characteristics

Although parrots differ markedly from one another in size and
coloring, they have many common characteristics. Particularly
noteworthy is the strongly curved, mobile beak, which, together
with the feet, is used by many parrots for climbing. Also characteristic is the climbing foot with four powerful claw-armed toes,
two of which face forward and two toward the back.

### Parrots in the Wild

Parrots are social animals. There are scarcely any loners among
them. Indeed, most species live in what are probably lifelong
monogamous relationships. Except during the brooding period,
almost all parrots join together in more or less gigantic flocks.
The natural food of parrots consists primarily of assorted plant
material, such as various fruits and seeds, buds, flower nectar,
and flower pollen, as well as worms, insect larvae, and grains
of sand (a mechanical digestive aid).

Parrots—depending on the species—lay 2 to 5 eggs, which
are usually brooded by the female alone. Some cockatoo species are the exception; in these the male also takes an active
part in the brooding. Brooding is done almost exclusively in
hollows of trees or branches, where the wood rot available
there frequently serves as the bottom of the nest. Only the
quaker parakeet builds a freestanding nest, and some lovebird
species pack existing hollow spaces with nesting material. Newly
hatched baby parrots are blind and almost completely naked. In
the beginning they are fed by the mother alone, and after 2 or
3 weeks by the father as well.

### Care

A fundamental concept of proper parrot care is that the birds be
kept in pairs, and encouraged to breed. Increased breeding
can, in the foreseeable future, eliminate the need for capture.
No species is suited to be kept in a cage exclusively. A compro-
mise is to keep the birds in a room cage and provide *supervised*
free flight, because parrots with strong beaks can gnaw furniture,
mouldings, and electric cords. Housing in an outdoor aviary is
the ideal. Sun and rain have a beneficial effect on the birds'
health and the condition of their plumage. An interior room that
can be closed off from the flight cage must be heated, with the
temperature regulated according to the birds' requirements.
Some parrots, such as lovebirds, use their nesting holes as
roosting places all year long. Most of the other species should

be provided with artificial nesting holes sometime in April. Only a few species introduce their own nesting materials; for most of them it is enough to spread the floor with a layer of slightly dampened wood shavings.

Many species can be fed well with commercially available seed mixtures. However, it is a good idea—at least during brooding and the raising of the young—to give them sprouted or at least soaked corn feed. A protein-rich brooding feed is also advisable for most species. In addition, the animal should always be offered a choice of fruit and green food. Vitamin and mineral supplements are also necessary.

**Parrot Keeping and the Law**

The Washington Endangered Species Agreement that went into effect in 1973 regulates the international trade in endangered animal and plant species. All parrot species with the exception of budgerigars, cockatiels, and ring-necked parakeets are covered by these regulations. The agency for carrying out the regulations in the U.S.A. is the USDA. In addition, the U.S. Department of the Interior rules require an inspection of imported birds and quarantine stations by its officials to ensure that the birds are not in the rare or endangered species category, are not illegally imported migratory birds, and are not agricultural pests or injurious to humans. For further details contact: Import-Export Staff Veterinary Services, APHIS U.S. Department of Agriculture, Hyattville, Maryland 20782

# Parrots Index

English translation © Copyright 1990
by Barron's Educational Series, Inc.

© Copyright 1988 by Gräfe and Unzer
GmbH, Munich, West Germany
The title of the German book is *Papageien und Sittiche*

Translated from the German by Elizabeth D. Crawford
Consulting Editor: Matthew M. Vriends, Ph.D.

All inquiries should be addressed to:
Barron's Educational Series, Inc.
250 Wireless Boulevard
Hauppauge, NY 11788

Library of Congress Catalog Card No. 90-465

International Standard Book No. 0-8120-4448-7

**Library of Congress Cataloging-in-Publication Data**

Kolar, Kurt.
    [Papageien und Sittiche. English]
    Parrots: a mini fact finder/Kurt Kolar.
        p.   cm.
    Translation of: Papageien und Sittiche.
    ISBN 0-8120-4448-7
    1. Parrots. I. Title.
SF473.P3K6513   1989                    90-465
636.6'865—dc20                          CIP

PRINTED IN HONG KONG

0123   9927      987654321

**Photo credits:** Angermayer: 43, inside front cover (1); ARDEA: 17 (Avon), 36 (Avon), 41 (Avon), 50 (Greensmith); Dossenbach: 8, 24, 26; Hosking: 20, 31, 37, 38, 44, 47, 49, 52, 55, 60; Reinhard: 12, 13, 21, 23, 25, 28, 33, 39, 45, 54, 58 inside front cover (4), back cover; Scholtz: 7, 9, 10, 11, 14, 15, 16, 18, 19, 22, 27, 29, 30, 32, 34, 35, 40, 46, 48, 51, 53; Skogstad: 3, 4, 5, 6, 57, 59, front cover; Wothe: 42, 56, inside front cover (1).